PENGUIN BOOKS

LAUREATE'S BLOCK

Tony Harrison was born in Leeds in 1937. He now lives in Newcastle upon Tyne. His collections of poetry include *The Loiners*, which won the Geoffrey Faber Memorial Prize in 1972; *Continuous*; *v.*, which was broadcast on Channel 4 in 1987, winning the Royal Television Society Award; *A Cold Coming* (Gulf War poems written for the *Guardian*); *The Gaze of the Gorgon* (Bloodaxe Books), which won the Whitbread Poetry Prize in 1992; and *Selected Poems* (third edition, Penguin 1995). He also contributed a selection of poems to Volume 5 of the *Penguin Modern Poets* series. Two audio cassettes of Tony Harrison reading selections of his poems have been released, one, *v. and Other Poems*, in 1997 by Penguin/Faber & Faber, and a second in 1998 by Bloodaxe Books.

Recognized as Britain's leading theatre and film poet, Tony Harrison has written extensively for the National Theatre, the New York Metropolitan Opera, the BBC and Channel 4. His *Dramatic Verse 1973–1985* (Bloodaxe Books) collects verse drama, opera libretti and music theatre, including his National Theatre version of Aeschylus's *Oresteia*, which won the European Poetry Translation Prize in 1982. *The Mysteries* (Faber), his acclaimed adaptation of the medieval English Mystery Plays, premièred at the National Theatre in 1985 and is being revived for the millennium, and his play, *The Trackers of Oxyrhynchus*, which was directed by the poet, was first performed in the ancient stadium of Delphi in 1988, appeared at the National Theatre in 1990 and also toured in Europe. *Square Rounds*, his original play for the National Theatre, had its première in 1992. Since then he has written and directed three new plays at special performance spaces: *Poetry or Bust* (Salts Mill, Saltaire, Yorkshire; 1993), *The Kaisers of Carnuntum* (the ancient Roman amphitheatre Carnuntum, Austria; 1995) and *The Labours of Herakles* (on the hillside site for the new theatre of Delphi, Greece; 1995). These are published as *Plays 3* by Faber & Faber (1996), who also publish his new translation of Victor Hugo's *The Prince's Play*, which opened at the National Theatre in April 1996.

Among his many television films are *Arctic Paradise*, *The Big H*, the four-part BBC series *Loving Memory*, and his film poems, *The Blasphemers' Banquet* and *The Gaze of the Gorgon*. His film *Black Daisies for the Bride* won the Prix Italia in 1994 and an award from the Mental Health Media. His film/poem *A Maybe Day in Kazakhstan* was specially commissioned for the anniversary of democracy in 1994 and *The Shadow of Hiroshima* for the fiftieth anniversary of the destruction of Hiroshima in 1995. His film/poem texts are collected in *The Shadow of Hiroshima and Other Film Poems* (Faber, 1995), which won the 1996 William Heinemann Prize. In 1995 he was sent by the *Guardian* to Bosnia and he wrote poems on the conflict for the front page. His first feature film, *Prometheus*, written and directed by the poet, went on general release in 1999. The screenplay is published by Faber & Faber.

Laureate's Block

TONY HARRISON

PENGUIN BOOKS

PENGUIN BOOKS

Published by the Penguin Group
Penguin Books Ltd, 27 Wrights Lane, London W8 5TZ, England
Penguin Putnam Inc., 375 Hudson Street, New York, New York 10014, USA
Penguin Books Australia Ltd, Ringwood, Victoria, Australia
Penguin Books Canada Ltd, 10 Alcorn Avenue, Toronto, Ontario, Canada M4V 3B2
Penguin Books (NZ) Ltd, Private Bag 102902, NSMC, Auckland, New Zealand

Penguin Books Ltd, Registered Offices: Harmondsworth, Middlesex, England

First published 2000
10 9 8 7 6 5 4 3 2 1

Some of these poems first appeared in the *Guardian*, the *London Review of Books*, *Tony Harrison: Loiner* (ed. Sandie Byrne, Clarendon Press, Oxford, 1997), *Changing Faces* (ed. Janet Prowting, Oberon Books, 1997), the *New Statesman* and *Poetry Review*

Set in Monotype Sabon
Typeset by Rowland Phototypesetting Ltd,
Bury St Edmunds, Suffolk
Printed in England by Clays Ltd, St Ives plc

Contents

A Celebratory Ode on the Abdication of King Charles III

It's not surprising that the Muse
has had to bypass Laureate Hughes
and chooses me to be the bard
to hymn the close of this charade,
and hymn the Crown's demise I will
with this black goose-feather quill
I've saved for ages just to write:
Goodbye! Good riddance, Divine Right!
and anything that still pretends
divinity shapes human ends.
No *Fidei Defensor* now can guard
the worn-out Church from knacker's yard.

First with its feather end I'll dust
the eyeballs of the Milton bust
I've kept as a constant inspiration
towards a now maturer nation,
Milton, whose Latin justified
to Europe Britain's regicide,
with his blind and marble eyes
sheds no tears for this demise.
We only weep we had to wait

so long to have an adult state.
Why has it taken all this while
desceptring 'this sceptred isle'?

Between Charles I and II
Britain had a chance she blew.
Britain blew her biggest chance
to be a grown-up girl like France
but history has cried FINIS
and drawn a line at King Charles III.
Britain's watched as waves have swept her
last King with his crown and sceptre
into the tides of change Canute
saw lapping at his well-licked boot.
Though later kings chose to ignore
the breakers crashing on the shore
that leave poor Charles's ermine sodden
with the momentum of the modern.

More democratic, more adult
with no mystique of monarch cult,
let's begin by hauling down
the Rs in names that mean the Crown,
the R from every acronym
that's lost its use along with him.

2

Remove that R that's everywhere!
First, you, my friend (Sir?) Richard Eyre
take that R from R N T
always a sore point with me
so I'm the first to shout hurrah
that the National's free to drop its R.
They claimed the added R would raise
much needed cash much more than plays.
'It gave us dignity abroad'
according to Chairman Rayne (now Lord!)
I beg to differ, *au contraire*,
we just seem backward everywhere.
All that bowing to the Royal Box
just makes us into laughing stocks.
From now on let our stage creation
be simply offered to the nation
and none of us need now be forced
to be so royally endorsed.
Now work should seem its own reward
to every would-be Sir or Lord
and all those former Sirs and Dames
will be content with simple names
without a prefix or a suf-.
In a republic work's enough.
Hopefully the day is dawning
when Britons lose their taste for fawning

on Lords and Ladies, Dames and Knights
dubbed by bepurpled parasites
and will demand a Bill of Rights.
A UK with a prefix 'Former'
sends tiaras into trauma
but *King*-dom's nothing when the King
's been taken under history's wing.
It's probably just British luck
the acronym comes out as FUK!

Now finally we've cast aside
the monarch without regicide.
It's 'off with his crown' instead
of, as before, 'off with his head'!
And he's agreed all by himself
to put the crown on to the shelf
where it must for ever stay
except for V&A display.

If Britain goes back where she was
and Republicans all flee to Oz
and there's a new ode to be written
to welcome King Charles back to Britain
I rather fear the Royal Muse
will have to go to Laureate Hughes.
An 'Ode on Monarchy Restored'
could make a Laureate a Lord.

Deathwatch Danceathon

Six centuries of insect sex
make hallowed rafters hollow wrecks,
the high and holy upheld by
oak-beams gnawed to casks of ply,
and their *Totentanz* tattoos
percussive in half-empty pews
are sex-sex-sex, the tapping crown
of cruising bug brings churches down.

How many houses for the Lord
has the knock-for-nooky squatter gnawed?
Carved escutcheon, scuncheon-squatters
more bug cloggies than gavotters,
rafter-feasters, roodscreen-wreckers
send morse-a-mate from mite maracas.
In oak as old as Robin Hood
the midnight maters knock on wood.

The male bug's tappings telegraph to
every female in the rafter,
11 times per second beat
the insect 42nd St
and oak-feasters' Easter Parade's
booming in old balustrades,

and the sick man in the bed below
hears the knock-tease to and fro.

The mortal patient in the bed
hears their mating call with dread.
He hears the termite dancers tapping
tattoos that terminate in tupping,
the Deathwatch Beetle like Blind Pew
groping towards his rendezvous
and that dry staccato sound
brings old institutions to the ground.

Beetle bonkers in the beams
spell the end of old regimes.
Down come beams and joists and doors
to the foreplay of the xylovores,
ancient truss and cruck
cracked by fronsaphonic fuck.
Bluntly put the bugger's fucked yer
entire infested infrastructure.

Devourers of dead wood supports
of mansions, palaces and courts,
each fat white grub will have gnawed a
good few yards of Old World Order.
The rat-a-tat-tat of rafter roaches
tapping their sexual approaches,

a frolic of phallic infestation
expected in a monarch nation.

Old palaces, old churches, courts
with rotting tap-schools for supports,
sex-mad rafter-hopping hordes
in chapel panel, west-wing boards.
In the end the bug brings down
the bedpost carved with shield and crown
and goes on dining and makes fall
the portrait-laden palace wall.

Other lives get nourished by
the sick man who's about to die.
On Ilka Moor Baht 'at
declares: man's himself a habitat
where worm and duck and fellow Tyke'll
help complete the foodchain cycle.
So don't imagine it's all gloom
to hear the deathwatch in the room.

The mortal summons in the wall's
some other creature's mating calls,
sending a rhythm along the beams
the spells the end of old regimes.
And the fruitful female bears
a future horde of new Astaires,

each a tuneful tapping trouper
part Gene Kelly, part Gene Krupa.

Gilt cherubs once with chubby cheeks
look down now like noseless freaks.
Like stuffing from a teddy bear
their wooden innards fill the air,
little motes of carven oak
with brief puffs of a golden smoke,
golden *putti* tiny specks
of oak confetti for mite sex.

The wooden saintling wondreth whither
cometh the knock-knock-knock come-hither,
from his brain or from his heart
or from some other uncarved part.
Sawdust created by no saw
but sexaphonic xylovore,
their friable physique now floats
as dancing, dull or golden motes.

The momentum of this very verse
drums up the stretcher and the hearse,
a beat that comes from long before
the King-beheading Civil War
divided still divided Britain
and Andrew Marvell's poem got written

(though now he'd say that at his back
trotted ghost-writer Pasternak!).

So 'never send' and 'had we but'
and such like thoughts sublimely put
by poets who've used the tolling bell
to cast an otherworldly spell,
or 'time's winged chariot' as a ploy
to make a mistress act less coy.
Put less ornately 'we're soon dead,
my sweetest darling, come to bed!'

So lovers lie, listening to taps,
part copulation, part collapse,
the mortal summons in the wall
that's just some creature's mating call –
Eros/Thanatos a pair
like Ginger Rogers/Fred Astaire,
one figure fleshless and one full,
the dancing duo, cheek to skull.

The very verse the poet employed
to make the virgin see the void
and be thus vertiginously sped
into Andrew Marvell's bed,
is the beat whose very ictus
turns smiling kiss to smirking rictus,

the urgent beat that wipes away
the urgency of what poems say.

Like the car and house alarms
that lovers in each other's arms
hear going off and left to bleep
the neighbourhood from love and sleep,
piercing, pulsating throbbers
disturbing everyone but robbers.
Everywhere there is a measure
heard or unheard of our pleasure.

Two pulses slightly out of synch,
flexi-phials of coursing *Quink*,
the metred couplet with its rhyme
revels in and coasts on time
we haven't got enough of – there
beneath the gently lifted hair
the artery that keeps repeating
life and its ending in one beating.

And in a palace's four-poster where
deathwatch dustmotes fill the air
in the densest dancing cloud
the beetle's drumming is most loud.
In Kensington he makes a killing,
the Deathwatch Beetle, drumming, drilling,

head in and out the polished oak
leaves one last prick-hole as they poke –

Their 'grubby' passion, his and hers,
spurned, pampered Princess, squire in spurs,
and as four-poster bedposts rock
we hear the deathwatch: knock . . . knock . . .
    knock . . .
and though too gentle for the axe
quicker than Anna Pasternak's,
I think, with Andrew Marvell, I can hear
the gavel of the auctioneer . . .

(The Deathwatch geigering for fucks
leaves the book worm to the books!)

Laureate's Block

FOR QUEEN ELIZABETH

I'm appalled to see newspapers use my name
as 'widely tipped' for a job I'd never seek.
Swans come in Domestic, Mute, and Tame
and no swan-upper's going to nick my beak

I'm particularly vexed that it occurred
in those same Guardian *pages where I'd written*
on the abdication of King Charles III
in the hope of a republic in Great Britain.

I wrote the above last night but what comes next
I wrote the day that Ted Hughes, sadly, died
and to exit from the lists I've faxed the text
for inclusion in the Guardian *(op.ed side?):*

No doubt inspired by the lunchtime news
the salesman, passing volumes by myself,
was selecting all the second-hand Ted Hughes
to move to the window from the poetry shelf.

A poet's death fills other poets with dread,
timor mortis like Dunbar's, and of the fate

of being remaindered, and not ever read,
but this bookshop window's got *Crow* laid in state,

with front cover showing now not just the spine.
At least they get your books out on display.
I'm doubting that they'll bother much with mine,
as I buy an old 4-volume Thomas Gray.

It was in this Stratford bookshop that I heard
Ted died, and needed my lover, stuck on stage
as Queen Elizabeth in *Richard III*,
to help me not to brood I'm near Ted's age.

While she ran the gauntlet of gut-curdling guile
child murder, mayhem, lust for monarchy
I walked by the swollen Avon for a while.
The plastic bag with Gray in banged my knee.

The swans' feet were slapping on deep towpath mud.
They wouldn't venture on the Avon out of fear
of the overflowing river in full flood
and getting their necks wrung dragged into the weir.

While my lover had to do two *Richard III*'s
I went to bed and read from front to back
all those four vols of Gray and found these words:
the saponaceous qualities of sack

in a letter that I think's worth perusal
especially by unversed journalists
who speculate which poet after Hughes'll
get a post Gray wouldn't credit still exists.

Though I could, because I've practised, paraphrase
in his *Elegy*'s quatrains if I so chose,
the following remarks of Thomas Gray's.
I'll quote them as he wrote them in plain prose:

*Though I very well know the bland emollient sapona-
ceous qualities of sack and silver, yet if any great man
would say to me 'I make you rat-catcher to his Majesty,
with a salary of £300 a year and two butts of the best
Malaga; and though it has been usual to catch a mouse
or two, for form's sake, in public once a year, yet to
you, sir, we shall not stand upon these things' I cannot
say I should jump at it, nay, if they would drop the very
name of the office, and call me Sinecure to the King's
Majesty, I should still feel a little awkward, and think
everybody I saw smelt a rat about me . . .*

*The office itself has always humbled the professor
hitherto (even in an age when kings were somebody), if
he were a poor writer by making him more conspicu-
ous, and if he were a good one by setting him at war*

with the little fry of his own profession, for there are
poets little enough to envy even a poet laureat.

(Dec 19, 1757)

That's Gray 2 centuries and more ago
with sentiments I find quite close to my mine.
And anyone who knew my work would know
which words of Thomas Gray I'd underline.

And the new rat-catcher to our present Queen,
who must have palace rodents sleek and fat,
though he/she washes after catches and keeps clean,
still sports retainer's raiment rank with rat.

There should be no successor to Ted Hughes.
'The saponaceous qualities of sack'
are purest poison if paid poets lose
their freedom as PM's or monarch's hack.

Nor should Prince Charles succeed our present Queen
and spare us some toad's ode on coronation.
I'd like all suchlike odes there've ever been
binned by a truly democratic nation.

Are there poets who are monarchists who'll try?
They might well get a Garter for their guts.

You'll never hear me heave an envious sigh.
I'd sooner be a free man with no butts,

free not to have to puff some prince's wedding,
free to say up yours to Tony Blair,
to write an ode on Charles I's beheading
and regret the restoration of his heir

(I'd hoped last week that would-be royal hacks
that self-promoting sycophantic flock
would whet their talents on the headman's axe
but it seems like a bad case of laureate's block —

30 January 1649
though it's hard to use the date for self-promotion
the anniversary's gone by with not a line
from toadies like Di-deifying Motion),

free to write what I think should be written,
free to scatter scorn on Number 10,
free to blast and bollock Blairite Britain
(and alliterate outrageously like then!)

free to write exactly as I choose
and heed both Thomas Gray's and Milton's ghost.
It's not for Laureate poems we'll miss Ted Hughes
nor any past pretender to the post.

And free, once Richard's off and Richmond's on
the battered throne with hacked crown on his head
and widowed women wan and wobegone,
when my unpainted queen's back in our bed,

to kiss my dedication, hot with scenes
of regal wrath, rage, wrangle, kiss away,
as we kiss equals and do not kiss queens,
the bitter taste of Shakespeare's bloody play.

A poet's death fills other poets with dread,
a king's death kings, but under my duvet
is Queen Elizabeth, and off our bed
slide these quatrains and all of Thomas Gray.

[untitled]

FOR RICHARD EYRE

You'd so brilliantly directed what I wrote
with our anti-royal ranter centre-stage
that I re-read *The Prince's Play* to find a quote
to gloss my mugshot on the facing page,
but, reluctantly, decided in the end
that the lines that I liked most weren't any use –

How could I shower my newly knighted friend
with all that deeply felt republican abuse?

English Opera

Sir Harry
Sir Gawain
Surtitles!

THREE POEMS FROM BOSNIA

1] *The Cycles of Donji Vakuf*

We take *Emerald* to Bugojno, then the *Opal* route
to Donji Vakuf where Kalashnikovs still shoot
at retreating Serbs or at the sky
to drum up the leaden beat of victory.
Once more, though this time Serbian, homes
get pounded to façades like honeycombs.
This time it's the Bosnian Muslims' turn
to 'cleanse' a taken town, to loot, and burn
Donji Vakuf fell last night at 11.
Victory's signalled by firing rounds to Heaven
and for the god to whom their victory's owed.
We see some victors cycling down the road
on bikes that they're too big for. They feel so tall
as victors, all conveyances seem small,
but one, whose knees keep bumping on his chin,
rides a kid's cycle, with a mandolin,
also childish size, strapped to the saddle,
jogging against him as he tries to pedal.
His machine gun and the mandolin impede
his furious pedalling, and slow down the speed

appropriate to victors, huge-limbed and big-booted,
and he's defeated by the small bike that he's looted.

The luckiest looters come down dragging cattle,
two and three apiece they've won in battle.
A goat whose udder seems about to burst
squirts her milk to quench a victor's thirst
which others quench with a shared beer, as a cow,
who's no idea she's a Muslim's now,
sprays a triumphal arch of piss across
the path of her new happy Bosnian boss.
Another struggles with stuffed rucksack, gun, and bike,
small and red, he knows his kid will like,
and he hands me his Kalashnikov to hold
to free his hands. Rain makes it wet and cold.
When he's balanced his booty, he makes off,
for a moment forgetting his Kalashnikov,
which he slings with all his looted load
on to his shoulder, and trudges down the road
where a solitary reaper passes by,
scythe on his shoulder, wanting fields to dry,
hoping, listening to the thunder, that the day
will brighten up enough to cut his hay.

And tonight some small boy will be glad
he's got the present of a bike from soldier dad,

who braved the Serb artillery and fire
to bring back a scuffed red bike with one flat tyre.
And among the thousands fleeing north, another
with all his gladness gutted, with his mother,
knowing the nightmare they are cycling in,
will miss the music of his mandolin.

Donji Vakuf
14 September 1995

11]   *The Bright Lights of Sarajevo*

After the hours that Sarajevans pass
queuing with empty canisters of gas
to get the refills they wheel home in prams,
or queuing for the precious meagre grams
of bread they're rationed to each day,
and often dodging snipers on the way,
or struggling up sometimes eleven flights
of stairs with water, then you'd think that the nights
of Sarajevo would be totally devoid
of people walking streets Serb shells destroyed,
but tonight in Sarajevo that's just not the case –

The young go walking at a stroller's pace,
black shapes impossible to mark
as Muslim, Serb or Croat in such dark.
In unlit streets you can't distinguish who
calls bread *hjleb* or *hleb* or calls it *kruh*.
All take the evening air with stroller's stride,
no torches guide them but they don't collide
except as one of the flirtatious ploys
when a girl's dark shape is fancied by some boy's.

Then the tender radar of the tone of voice
shows by its signals she approves his choice.

Then match or lighter to a cigarette
to check in her eyes if he's made progress yet.

And I see a pair who've certainly progressed
beyond the tone of voice and match flare test
and he's about, I think, to take her hand
and lead her away from where they stand
on two shell splash scars, where in '92
Serb mortars massacred the breadshop queue
and blood-dunked crusts of shredded bread
lay on the pavement with the broken dead.
And at their feet in holes made by the mortar
that caused the massacre, now full of water
from the rain that's poured down half the day,
though now even the smallest clouds have cleared
     away,
leaving the Sarajevo star-filled evening sky
ideally bright and clear for bomber's eye,
in those two rain-full shell-holes the boy sees
fragments of the splintered Pleiades,
sprinkled on those death-deep, death-dark wells
splashed on the pavement by Serb mortar shells.

The dark boy shape leads dark girl shape away
to share one coffee in a candlelit café

until the curfew, and he holds her hand
behind AID flour sacks refilled with sand.

Sarajevo
20 September 1995

III]   *Essentials*

(Conversation with a Croat)

'I looked at my Shakespeares and said NO!
I looked at my Sartres, which I often read
by candlelight, and couldn't let them go
even at this time of direst need.

Because he was a Fascist like our *Chetnik* foes
I lingered for a while at my Célines . . .
but he's such a serious stylist, so I chose
Das Kapital to cook my AID canned beans!'

Sarajevo
20 September 1995

26

TWO POEMS FOR MY SON IN HIS SICKNESS

I]   *Rice-Paper Man*

i]

Anything, or almost, 's worth at least a try.
Lifelong rationalists, afraid to die,
shuffle shiftily to 'healers', often lurch
from chemotherapy back to the church.
When, if I fall ill, things get that bad,
I'll try to stand by reason. As a dad,
I have to say, there've been times when I've done
deeds I hate confessing, for my son.
I never pray; I scorn religious quacks
but do things I despise, for my son, Max,
out of unbearable panic at his pain:
like light a candle in a church in Spain.

ii]

On either side were grim *memento mori*
by Valdes Leal: *The End of the World's Glory*,
and Death with a scythe: *In Ictu Oculi*
(English: *In the Twinkling of an Eye*),

that blink that makes smooth bishops and rough bums
lie clasped in the charnel like close bosom chums.
Here Death glides by as if on rollerblades
over disarrays of books, maps, red brocades,
unplucked violas, and goes on to spin
a globe with now 6 billion people in.
The monarch *esqueletto* squats
on piles of skulls ten billion times Pol Pot's.

iii]

The church is near the bullring and *olé*s
keep breaking in on my despairing daze.
In Ictu Oculi! I hear crowd roars
at *torero*'s coup de grâce or *toro*'s gores.
In Ictu Oculi! Each loud *olé*
cheers scything *esqueletto* on his way,
a match for both the bull and brave bullfighter,
casual crusher of crozier and mitre,
serial suffocator, who can snuff
the most brilliant suit of lights with just one puff.
Death trashes all. The minute that we're born's
the moment *toro Tod* dips his honed horns.

iv]

Dereliction, death, decay, *olé! olé!*
images designed to make you pray.

I light a candle. The paintings say we die,
but don't recover 'in the twinkling of an eye'.
All that Death in triumph can induce
a taste for lighting candles. No excuse!
And it gets worse. The next thing was the day
at Bran I flung my loose Romanian *lei*
into Vlad the Impaler's castle well,
and made a wish: *please free Max from his hell.*
Asking Dracula! How slippery the slope
when a despairing man runs out of hope.

v]

The third thing was this last year in Japan
trying a temple shrine's rice-paper man.
From bad to worse. The third thing that I've done,
so desperate and despairing for my son,
is drop 200 yen into a box and buy
a small rice-paper man to give a try.
You scribble the sickness on the mannikin
on whatever part the pain or trouble's in
and drop it in the temple pail. With me
it'd be my chronic shoulder or arthritic knee,
or heartache. For his specific form of pain
the word's too big to write across its brain.

vi]

One rice-paper man! I'd have to scrawl
his sickness on hundreds if I wrote it all,
without the skills of Signor Cossovel
who micrographically wrote Dante's *Hell*,
and *Purgatory* AND *Paradise*,
not on a mannikin made out of rice,
but (I've *seen* it in Ravenna!) on one sheet
of A3 paper in 1888.
The shock of seeing his wee *figlio* die
left him with hyperaesthesia of the eye,
which condition allowed him to condense,
the entire *Commedia* without a lens.

vii]

So I write the diagnosis and that's all –
schizophrenia's hard to fit in even small.
It started with the head that bowed and curled
to hide from the constant terrors of the world.
The head rolls downwards like a curling leaf,
the whole brain foetal in its fall of grief.
The dissolving man in pain's now like a worm,
then dull slug trail and, last, like cloudy sperm,
come in a loo bowl that won't ever know
the tragedy of man and all his woe.

Once the paper man's dissolved no eye could tell,
say, my arthritis from his mental hell.

viii]

Circles of hell and *Haliperidol*
Cossovel couldn't cram in one fat vol
let alone on one rice-paper man
the desperate put their faith in in Japan.
Cossovel got his skill when his wee lad,
his *figlioletto*, died. And mine's gone mad.
Though the terror didn't traumatize my sight,
the shock, like Cossovel's, forced me to write.
You may have other props but this is mine.
Follow me down this stairway, line by line,
solidarity in darkness, writer/reader,
tu mi segui, e io sarò tua guida.

ix]

A serene young monk in saffron silk
takes all the water suffering's made milk
or more opaque than milk, a spermy goo,
and swills it down a drain of dry bamboo,
then takes clear water from a dragon spout
that spews spring water not spit fire out,
and, waiting with bowed shaven head, refills
the bamboo bucket for tomorrow's ills.

Each little floating scapegoat's pain tattoo
will sink the swimmer that it bends in two.
And tomorrow there'll be new queues with their yen
loading their hopes on frail rice-paper men.

x]

When all you want to do's sit down and cry
anything, or almost, 's worth at least a try,
from Dracula's deep well in Castle Bran
to the temple pail I tried out in Japan.
Or is it, was it, when I have at my command
my mind, my heart, my guts, my writing hand?
My pen's no wand, and I'm no Prospero,
but poems are the one redemption that I know.
Anything with God in is the worst.
This last resort I should have fled to first.
Somewhere I always have to draw the line.
You have your own props and poetry's mine –

xi]

Poetry wasn't first because I go
to poetry whenever I feel low,
but by resorting to it O so many times
I've built up an immunity to rhymes.
My deliverance, the drive to shape,
that throws up no solutions nor escape,

that drive to shape, 's my son's destroyer,
the just as well wrought urn of paranoia.
Other poets' sons and daughters, Joyce's
Frost's and Victor Hugo's, all heard voices.
Is what tears our offsprings' minds apart
the shaping spirit of poetic art?

xii]

First came the hour-long candle in Seville,
with loud *olé*s, that left my son still ill,
second the silly well in Castle Bran
and last a bamboo bucket in Japan.
Great remedies! But not the last resort
which might have more in common than I thought
with those superstitious nonsenses above,
springing as all do from fear and love,
the last resort is these words, that you read,
possibly yourself in desperate need.
I've tried to keep out all false hope, and lies,
that kill those quack concoctions I despise.

xiii]

We're all subject to the Cossovellian rule:
a loved one's pain makes epics minuscule,
and not just epics, I imagine his changed eyes
reduced all man esteems to micro size.

In Ictu Oculi, one little blink,
one little death makes even Dante shrink.
In Ictu Oculi! But just suppose,
in another sort of trauma, Dante grows
into manuscript constructed by Brunel,
alphabet bulk blocks bridging Earth and Hell,
one 's reductionist, and neither use
the true proportions of the human Muse.

xiv]

Poetry 's neither vast nor micro size.
I've shown you things I've done that I despise,
desperate for my son. I can't excuse
betraying my true, my truth-tormented Muse
who moves this poem that's coming to a close.
And what the hell 's its use in all our woes?
The question is: Do you think poetry,
specifically *this* poem, was worth a try?
If not, and you found no comfort, not one phrase
to brave *memento mori* and *olés*,
or redeem doomed spermatozoa, drive
a stake through this undead art and you'll survive.

11] *Sugaring the Pill*

In Africa I'd give you *Paludrine*
with guava jam to hide its tart taste in.

I poised above you in your netted pram
with malaria prophylactic mashed in jam.

I put the spoon near my mouth, said *yum-yum*
to persuade you that some treat's about to come.

Even so tiny, after once or twice, you knew
the performance of smacked lips just wasn't true.

The nets are down; our roles have been reversed
you take the bitterest pill and taste it first.

No malaria then, but later much, much worse
too full of gall to swallow even mashed in verse.

FOUR POEMS FOR JONATHAN
SILVER IN HIS SICKNESS

I]   *Auroras*

You gave me your *Aurora* pen,
something I'd never buy.
It had scented lilac ink in then,
now that lilac ink 's run dry.

That scented lilac ink 's run dry,
my *Aurora* 's filled with black,
though today I won't deny
I'd like some lilac back.

Aurora (as you know) means dawn
and you've ordered a new one.
May the shining gold get worn
with greeting each day's sun.

I hear the *Aurora* you gave me
scratch across the page
desperate to write some poetry
you can re-read in old age.

Not only do I love its flow,
its gold Greek key motif,
the *Aurora* 's the only way I know
to reach beyond our grief.

Let's both pick up *Auroras*
(with permanent black or nay)
and write that what's before us
is another dawning day,

when sometimes the gold nib will glow
and sometimes will look dull,
but either way our *Auroras* flow
because days are so full.

20 January 1997

11]   *Marie Mastat*

Painted *Marimastat* fore and aft,
the *Marimastat* is your craft.
The *Marimastat* was a yacht
that Marie Mastat sailed a lot.
Marie Mastat, Balkan diva,
walking with her black retriever
that, on the cliff edge, wags its tail
to see the *Marimastat* sail.
And the sea song that you'll hear
is Marie Mastat's whose career
burgeoned first in Bucharest
and *every*body knows the rest –
the legendary vocal chords
vibrating as the world applauds!
She gave the yacht her name because,
her voice not being what it was,
she said that 'given the right breeze'
she still could venture on high Cs.

They also named a sweet brown wine
Marie Mastat (a Murfatlar vine
found near the Danube and Black Sea)
the diva passes off as tea

as she lolls in her *conservatoire*,
Marie Mastat, Balkan star,
smoking a black cigarette
among mementos of the Met,
and each smoke ring that she blows
turns into a Yorkshire rose
she tosses at her dearest fan,
a venturer called Jonathan,
who with the rose between his teeth
and the *Marimastat*'s deck beneath,
sails towards the next Aurora
with Marie's ghost as his wine-pourer.
And on the high seas Marie's ghost
pours *Marie Mastat* for a toast
to Jonathan, who her ghost guides
through the night-times and the tides.
The label peeling off the bottle
shows the diva in full throttle,
the mouth wide, about to pour a
cascade of high Cs for Aurora.

The *Marimastat* spreads her sails.
Marie's ghost goes through her scales,
and, when storms brew or when night falls,
sings arias through dark and squalls,

and her voice will summon from the shore a
lifeboat with the name: AURORA.

2 February 1997

(Note: *Marimastat* was a new drug in trials
for cancer treatment.)

III] *Valetudinous Valentine*

FOR JONATHAN AND MAGGIE

Better than red roses and red hearts,
today a new tradition starts.
Every Valentine's from now
we'll all of us remember how
Jonathan Silver of Salts Mill,
when popping his first small pink pill
discovered the right course to follow
to guarantee long life is swallow
the initial dosage of the drug
with Aurora-toasting vintage KRUG.

14 February 1997

IV] *Border Honey*

She tends her border hives and sings.
   She gives me honey wax to chew
   to stave off hunger till we're through
and dabs vinegar on my five stings.
She yelled the price in *lev* and *lei*
   over the deep hum of the swarm
   and poured the honey thick and warm
into this bottle that I bring today,
to sweeten your sustaining tea.
   The border I brought it from took hours
   crossing, but both the states' sunflowers
stretched as far as the eye could see.

Both sides the tailback border bees
   through yellow, dwarfing most of us,
   first browse Romania's then buzz
Bulgaria's with stateless ease.
When David H. feared you might die
   he painted sunflowers for you
   'for hope and joy' when you came through
and brought the canvas still not dry.
So that, when they wheeled you back

42

from cancer surgery, you'd get
     the sunflowers he brought them wet
with petals printed on his mac.

A Bulgarian barrier blocks the way
     and for guards to let the cursing queue,
     cars, trucks, and bullock wagons, through
took almost the whole bloody day,
with time at least to sleep and rest
     and time to sense the moving sun
     turn millions of heads as one
by slow degrees towards the West.
I queued and took snap after snap
     but the guard, with nothing else to do,
     ripped the new roll from my μ
to show he was a macho chap.

But the roll the guard did not destroy
     I laser-copied to A4
     and, like David's painted ones before,
bring *Sunflowers for Hope and Joy*,
to show how sweetnesses brought through
     more borders after those have come
     from flowers David's cadmium
under skies Matisse's blue.
And when it waits to cross, your soul,
     may border honey, from free bees

browsing both states' flowers, ease
your passage through control.

That viaticum from border hive,
the photographs I took for you,
brilliant yellow and bright blue,
you saw and tasted still alive.
On this side still how sad I am
this poem that went with them's late.
Because my verses imitate
the metre of In Memoriam,
they seemed too much an omen then
so I never gave the poem I'd penned
for hope and joy for my lost friend
with my (once his) Aurora pen.

IN MEMORIAM
JONATHAN SILVER (21.10.49–25.9.97)

Fruitility

What a glorious gift from Gaia
raspberries piled on papaya,
which as a ruse to lift my soul
I serve up in my breakfast bowl,
and, contemplating, celebrate
nature's fruit, and man's air-freight
speeding my fruit breakfast here
through tropo- and through stratosphere.
I praise papaya and celebrate
the man who packed it in its crate,
the worker or Hawaiian grower
in Kipahula or Pahoa,
the worried cultivator who
scans the sky from Honomu,
with global warming getting higher
than is good for his papaya;
worries I myself had known
when, in Nigeria, I'd grown
what we called pawpaws of my own;
picked, deseeded, served fridge-fresh
I fed my kids their orange flesh.
I gave my kids fruit to repeat
the way I once got fruit to eat,
not so exotic but the start

of all my wonder and my art.
My mother taught me to adore
the fruit she scrounged us in the War,
scarce, and marred with pock and wart
nonetheless the fruit she brought
taught me, very young, to savour
the gift of fruit, its flesh and flavour.
Adoring apples I've linked Eve's
with my mother's ripe James Grieves
no God could ever sour with sin
or jinx the juice all down my chin.
Still in my dreams my mother comes
her pinafore full of ripe plums,
Victorias, with amber ooze
round their stalks, and says: Choose! Choose!
Now so much older, I,
more aware I've got to die,
use such ruses, I derive
from my mother, to survive.
Last week I saw here at the Met
a 'Wheel of Life' made in Tibet
where 'Man Picking Fruit' 's used to depict,
in both the picker and the picked,
ultimate futility. Such dismal crap'll
never spoil my mother's apple.
Fuck philosophy that sees
life itself as some disease

we sicken with until released,
supervised by Pope or priest,
into a dry defruited zone
where no James Grieves were ever grown.
I'd barter nebulous Nirvanas
for carambolas or bananas.
I need to neologize to find
the fruit in futile humankind,
and *fruitility* is what I call
the fate which falls upon us all.
Meaningless our lives may be
but blessed with deep fruitility.
It could take pages if I list
all the joys of the fruitilitist:
retsina and grilled squid in Greece,
that death-bed cut-out of Matisse
I chanced on on a trip to Dallas,
Sempre libera sung by Callas,
love-making in the afternoon,
the ripe papaya on this spoon
lingered over as my way
of starting on a fruitile day,
where 73rd and Broadway meet.
Even now the morning heat
brings the piss smells off the street,
Dobermann's and man's piss soars
as far as us, and we're eight floors.

This breakfasting's my Zensual ruse
to counteract such Broadway views
as those below, where homeless spread
the books and mags to earn their bread
and, after bread, if not before,
the rocks of crack some value more.
I read titles with my opera glasses:
Opera News and *Chunky Asses*,
Honcho, *Ramrod*, *Newsweek*, *Time*,
stiff from showers 2 a dime,
but, if like new, then 4 a dollar,
Bush, the Pope, the Ayatollah,
Noriega, Gorbachev,
and other ones with covers off,
a *danse macabre*, a *Vanitas*
of big cheeses, and the chunky ass.
Diva-adoring gays peruse
the laid out rows of *Opera News*.
Spectacles of temporal flux,
sidewalk piles of grubby books,
30 copies of one play
billed a great hit in its day,
and some still supposed to be
a dollar each, or 4 for 3.
And there's a neighbour off to buy
the opera discs that help him die.

He's young but shuffles with a cane
but will only use CDs for pain.
His father, who won't meet him, mails
his sick son clothes from car-boot sales,
but Pa and Ma don't realize
AIDS makes their son a smaller size.
They've never talked of death or sex
but occasionally Pa sends him cheques
to buy AZT, as AZT's
one drug that slows down the disease.
I saw him in the lobby:
                              Hi,
Pa sent me some more cash to buy
AZT, but I bought these!
and showed me scores of new CDs.
My pa would think it such a waste
me and my opera ain't his taste.
Got all of Callas's CDs
to comfort me through this disease.
It's Puccini next when Pa sends more,
and he got off at the 7th floor . . .

There's someone wanting to be Mayor
haranguing winos in the square,
under Verdi's statue who presides
over crack-heads, crooks and suicides.
Verdi with his vision blurred

by birdshit stares from 73rd
down at Dante at the Met
where Verdi helps some to forget.
But when they leave or enter there
there's no avoiding Dante's stare,
nor what's beneath his constant gaze
and stays there, while the opera plays,
and pizza cartons three feet square
leave mouth-watering hot blasts of air,
a phantom mozzarella trail,
for carton dwellers to inhale
in lungfuls, hungry and alone
beyond the pale of *Pizzaphone*.
A claret goblet and WITH CARE
that housed video or frigidaire
now packages a shoeless man
who rummages the garbage can
already rummaged countless times
for cans you can redeem for dimes.
Shops redeem the empty can
but not the can-redeeming man,
nor that woman who's got business sense
so beds down where machines dispense
24hr cash, and men, when pissed,
might leave five dollars in her fist.
One night I saw a famous diva
stop her limo there and leave her

scores of fresh fan-flung bouquets
to wake to from her wino haze.
And when she woke they say she cried
with rage and terror, horrified
the morning sun should wake her
laid out for the undertaker.
Death was all these blooms could mean,
these tributes she was stretched between,
beneath the bank's cashpoint machine.
Once aware she wasn't dead
she flogged the star's bouquets for bread,
well, pretzels; those posh bouquets
kept her in booze for several days.

I dread the moment, while I muse
on all my fruitile 8th floor views,
I hear the answerphone replay
the dark side of the fruitile day:
message one, a Scottish friend,
sick, insomniac, half round the bend,
drying out in St Luke's, lying
all tubed-up, detoxifying.
His message goes as follows: *Hi!*
just checking in before I die!
The trolleyphone's beside his bed.
I call him back. He isn't dead.

Thought you were dying.
                    I am! I am!
Fucking dying for a dram!

Another friend made mad by A I D S
leaves night-time answerphone tirades.
It wakes us when the tape records
his rabid ravings from the wards.
First his operatic repertoire
that made him a tv bar star:
Sempre libera, in falsetto,
voice corseted as Violetta,
Sempre libera, always free,
he from A I D S and she T B.
In sigmoidoscopy he'd brag:
I am the world's most buggered fag
Your rooter's nothing, every dick
I've ever had's ten times as thick!
After the aria and the pause
while he curtsies to applause
and clasps flung posies to his heart
the mad Munchausen stories start
and I hear a new bass voice begin:

Those things like wine-stains on my skin
those fucking things like spilled Merlot
they ain't what you guys think you know.

They came, these scars like fucking Claret
from the forest of the flame-flayed parrot.
They're burns! They're burns! I tried to seize
the cure for AIDS from blazing trees.
I was in Brasil, Manaus, where I gave
my Violetta. And did Manaus rave!
They adore me, darlings, in Brasil.
They think I was just acting ill.
Brava! brava! on and on
beside the steaming Amazon.
If I chose I could earn millions
from brava-bravaing Brasilians!
(Were you aware the rubber trade's
booming again because of AIDS?
You see the stripe-gashed cauchos oozing
condoms I never packed when cruising!)
I went up-river in a cute caique
from Manaus with the urge to seek
the cure for what afflicts our kind
and the sights up river blew my mind –
I saw pink dolphins, pink!
and I hadn't had a drop to drink!
and no Colombia up my nose –
dolphins pink as any fan-flung rose!
I'd gone in costume. It was better
trekking dressed as Violetta.

Those creepers with sharp thorns don't snag
my depilated legs in drag.
And where the forest was ablaze,
brave Violetta, on behalf of gays,
in corsets botanizing raced
through dense forest now laid waste,
charcoal gallows, charcoal glades
of gutted antidotes for AIDS,
the canopy deserted by
the roasted birds that used to fly.
And there were cures. They've gone. They've gone
in the bonfires of the Amazon.
Some creeper, bud, some bitter seed
might be the breakthrough doctors need.
All September it's been blazing
to give more future Big Macs *grazing.*
Even now the forest flames
are burning cures that have no names.
In the ash of Amazonian oak
the cure for AIDS went up in smoke . . .

All this gabble seems quite graphic
though culled from *National Geographic*
bought at the sidewalk mag bazaar
with covers of the passé star
or politician laid between
Butt Lust 'Seat Meat' magazine

54

and iron pumping *Bulkritude*
both with pages wanker-glued.
Then his falsetto ends the story:

Cessarono gli spasimi del dolore . . .

The sun sets here while it's rising
on countries just industrializing
and day ends in a dying fire
hued like my rasps piled on papaya,
Broadway windows with glossed sheen
of cranberry and carotene,
sunset as the turning planet
paints New York in pomegranate,
with chemicals that now pollute
the skies to look like too ripe fruit.

The spoon-scraped limp papaya skin
goes first into the garbage bin,
then a big black trash bag, later
down the chute to the incinerator,
and the flotsam of time's fleeting flux
goes into dawn's first garbage trucks.
I'll hear them grinding as it's time
again for papaya spritzed with lime.
Tomorrow's rasps piled on papaya
chilled, ready for the life-denier,

tomorrow when my heart says *Yea*
to darkness ripening into day,
remembering my mother whose
gifts of fruit taught me this ruse,
whose wartime wisdom would embrace
both good and grotty with sweet grace,
she who always used to say:
Never wish your life away!
Of all my muses it was she
first taught me to love fruitility.

Toasting Jocelyn

A Toast on the 80th birthday of
Jocelyn Herbert

I'm getting up today to make a toast
to the person in my life I've toasted most,
and can't propose this toast unless I list
(and I *don't* mean all the times that we got pissed!)
those many toasts I've made when I've felt blessed
to know and work with someone who's the best.
And so before I raise this glass, dear Jocelyn,
these are some wines that you've been toasted in:

The first toast though was not in wine but beer
and the toast I made you then you didn't hear.
Long before our paths were, happily, to cross
I saw Ionesco's *Chairs* designed by Joc.
This play, some twenty years before we met,
was the first I'd seen in London, her first set.
Thrilled and elated by what I saw,
with half of bitter in the pub next door,
inspired, I made a silent toast, and thought:
Here's to George and Jocelyn and the Court!

How could I know then we had before us
the *Oresteia* that we played in Epidaurus.

And from that time there've been more than a few
magic moments when I've toasted you:

With five sheep roasting on a charcoal fire
in barrel retsina for the *Oresteia*.
What else? What else? Let's see! Let's see . . .
that strange Arachova rosé with *kokkoretsi*,
that strange Parnassus resinous rosé
in which I thanked you for our satyr play.

And by the Danube when the nightingale
sang for our satyrs after violent hail
flooded our whole set and you and I,
with a garden roller, rolled our desert dry,
then later when the stars began to shine
toasted each other in *Dreikaiserwein*.

Dreikaiserwein was once again the brew
in which I toasted all I owed to you,
when we mounted in Carnuntum such a sight
that still gives Viennese a sleepless night,
and I don't just mean the lions, tigers, bears,
prowling beneath the seating and the stairs,
but something far more scary and horrendous –

Barrie Rutter, in silk stockings and suspenders!

Or getting a taxi to Slovakia to have a
stroll round medieval Bratislava
and, with herby *Becherovka* and weak tea,
I toasted you in Slovak: *Nazdravi*!

Retsina, *Dreikaiserwein* and *Becherovka* . . . Shit!
(Excuse me!) I forgot the *Aquavit*
in Copenhagen when on tour with *Trackers*,
toasting our collaboration, and Lord Bacchus.

But in case you think us both obsessed with booze
I ought to say we've pledged the Tragic Muse
and Comic Muse, Melpomene and Thalia,
in the purest crystal waters of Castalia,
and when I dip my scooping palm and drink
at Castalia with Jocelyn I think
that she's been more inspiring than the Muse
and deserves from me a million ιασους.
And mostly I remember toasting you
in my favourite toast of all, the Greek ιασους!

And ιασου comes from one who can't be here
all the way to London from Itea.
Tsaros who catches and then cooks our favourite dish
γαριδες σαγανακι sends his birthday wish
and told me to say 'Come soon' and say a
loud ιασου from the Silenus of Itea.

Also Dionissis Fotopoulos
asked me to tell you that he loves you, Joc.
And is sending you, via Hermes, a bouquet
of herbs, picked in Delphi, on this very day.

This glass is the memory of those toasts
I've made on Greece's mountains and her coasts,
and the happiness of glasses still to raise
in all our future recces, films and plays.
For the toasting won't by any means stop here,
we've another big adventure on this year,
when I think that toasts will have to be
in Romanian *tuica* and Bulgarian *raki*,
until we'll end up saying ιασου in retsina
and that taverna by the docks in Elefsina.
So this glass I toast you with I poise
between all the work we've done and all the joys
and all the work and joys we've still to do
and say with all my heart: ιασου, ιασου!

It's impossible to make such heartfelt toasts
and not invite the most beloved of ghosts,
and as present here this evening as I am
are George and Lindsay, Tony, Ron, John, Sam . . .
and they're all here to do what we'll all do,
raise our glasses and thank God for you.

And now in (What's this wine?) . . . *Viña Mayor*
(don't think I've toasted you in this before) . . .
This glass of wine we all have in our hands
is from the fertile vine of love, and stands
for all the wines you've been and will be toasted in –

I love you, and I toast you: JOCELYN!

22 February 1997

Leavings

I think that's the last one gone behind the sink!

Though after every meal we wipe and sweep,
though every crack's sealed up, the kitchen clean,
no matter how particular we've been,
the cockroaches emerge once we're asleep,
and waking in the night to get a drink
I switch on the kitchen light and see them run
from their catches and (for them) rich hoards
behind the oven and the skirting boards,
all safe for another night-hunt; but for one.

Caught also by the suddenness of light
my dream attempts to scuttle back to sleep,
scatters in all directions, but part stays
betrayed by its hunger for its yesterdays
into futures with a blunted appetite
for tomorrows that are fresh but do not keep.
Love strews its leavings where the lean nights feed.
The scavengers we keep at bay with care,
those night-thoughts that gnaw days with manic greed,
at death, are going to gorge on all they need
from memory's disconnected frigidaire.

The mind skates round its own transparent walls,
though that restraints exist it's unaware,
thinking because it sees there's nothing there
between what we once were and what we are,
and, feasting on old love, too gorged to climb
the slithering steep slopes of see-through time,
I feel the full heart gets so far, then falls,
like this cockroach skidding in the cookie jar.

Rubbish

All my rubbish is discreetly bagged,
some heavy with indulgence, some lightweight.
Some sail through the air, and some get dragged,
clinking, down to the gap that was the gate.

I didn't move when roofers fixed my tiles
or when the builder came to point the wall;
with the window cleaner I swap nods and smiles
and don't budge from my littered desk at all,
so why, when two men cross my threadbare lawn
each Monday morning emptying my bins,
as if my refuse was exposed to scorn,
my garbage a glaring index to my sins,
do I bolt from my study and go hide?

I think the reason is I can't abide
being caught pen in hand as gloved men chuck
black plastic sacks of old drafts on their truck.

Passer

His knuckle tattoos say: *Nothing* and *Futile*:

I'll kick in his knackers, boot straight to his bollocks.
I'll twist his tackle, he'll not toss off tomorrow!
His nob'll be naff for wanking for weeks!

Sigurd of sickbursts, brew-belcher, *Brown Ale*r,
What *lot* or *dom* do such dickheads lust after?
Spewdom for starters, the Sat'day excesses
lack and lacunae in lad-lore and lager,
livid at life, lashing out in lads' lingo,
Newky Nirvanas, the nightly negations,
the doubled-up drunkard heaving his *humous*.

But soaks' slop 's sustaining to the spuggy survivor:
the spuggy picks over the piss-artist's spew,
the *passer* picks over the piss-artist's puke,
unsqueamish in Corfu at squid-rings in sick slosh,
never nauseous on North roads at Niagaras of *Newky*,
slices of carrot in school crayon sunbursts,
Tandoori and *Tennants*, late nosh and *Newky*
devoured in the dawnlight, sluiced on to sidewalks,
kebab bits and *Carlsberg* gob-cacked, cataracted,
slivers of sleevers from last midnight's mêlée

tested for taste just in case they were juicy.
There's no lust for poison in the spuggy's spare spirit.
It's flight-feather fodder, spew is for spuggies.

Over boulders of gneiss, the bust kneecaps of Lenin,
the star-gazing eyes of horizontaled old Stalins,
pecking places for the *passer* (posh Latin for spuggy)
berries that bounce off the cracked busts and bronzes,
red hawthorn, pyracantha, the fruits of the May.
Look there, though, the spuggy, Bede's old soul
     symbol,
dodging the juggernauts to banquet on boke-bits.
The spuggy's the spirit Bede saw in brief transit
from darkness to darkness via being as banquet.
The scrabbled Cyrillic spuggies leave with birdclawfeet
's nowt spirit-lifting, but nowt nay-saying neither.
Spuggies sing as the light lifts, serenade the sun's
     sinking.

All meadhalls are measured by men at their margins,
the glee by the gloomfast, the song by the silence,
Sprechgesang by splutterings, Strad string by stranglers,
Puccini by punch-ups, *Tosca* by torture,
Callas by cattleprods, kilowatts to the cunt,
violins by the violence, cellos by the chokings,
the cabaret by the carton, built in the Bull Ring,
the paean by piss-artists, the beercan berserker

barracking the bardic, putting the boot in,
cornflakes or kippers by cranking the rack cogs,
snap crackle pop with the same in some cellar,
Gloucester's eyes acted by such deeds done daily,
curtain calls by kids kipping on kerbsides.
The *scop* scours the ruins for scraps of lost rhythms.
He once wrote *The Ruin* but on his returning
The Ruin is ruined, the writing has rotted,
the penmanship perished in fungoids or flamemarks.
There's no going back to piece it together
he looks through the lacunae to see Leeds and London,
the sacked scriptoria marked Stasi–Top Secret.
The *scop* of *The Ruin* felt like the *passer
scop*, spuggy, *passer*, the sorrowful sparrow
condemned to rewriting the gaps in *The Ruin*.

The willow herb waves once more on the wallstones.
The scop's messy mss. slashed with lacunae,
rubbler hyphen rebuilder, a walker of wallstones,
the *Wreacca-scop* walking Rome's empire in ruins,
pig troughs inscribed IMPERATOR or DIVUS,
cannibalized columns from Corbridge now Christian
upholding church masonry not a Mithraeum.
You might well bewail, in the wattle/daub era,
the giants have built, but their buildings are broken.
If such great constructions should come to the ground,
barracks and bath-house go for a Burton,

it buttered the Brits up to crave their conversion,
made all things regarded vain, vanishing, frail.
Now Socialist strongholds collapse into commerce,
sold at streetmarkets collected as kitsch,
military medals a marketed melée.

Canta mihi aliquid. Nescio, inquit, cantare.

Now ask that Caedmon to sing the collapses,
the megaliths ruined like the Romans before them,

The *Wreacca* met Caedmon and said: Fuck off,
    Caedmon!
Now Caedmon couldn't say: Cunt! back, now could
    he?

Bridlington

Sitting for David Hockney

Him drawing those lines me composing these,
our breathing inside louder than the sea's.
York*ssshhh*ire . . . *ssshhh* . . . York*ssshhh*ire . . . *ssshhh*
    they say
the whispering waves of this last day of May.

Pebbles skimmed by two school-skiving kids
bounce on bulky waves that dawdle on to Brid's
bare beaches where a man shouts, 'Stay!'
to his disobedient dog who runs away,
the studio clock with its metallic tick,
the craftblade scratching on the charcoal stick,
the gulls' cries and the crows' dry caws
as I compose, stock-still, and David draws,
and Brid's grey ocean, lisping and then lush
shuffles into one long silent *ssshhh*!

Doncaster

I've noticed Donny's bridal gownshop's lights
are only on, in winter, Saturday nights.
Though window shopping for white wedding gear
's not done this coldest, darkest time of year,
maybe, the owner reckons, as they pass
those near-nude girls, reflected in the glass,
might remember his window's lacy white,
if they get pregnant from their date tonight.

In Donny at the *Danum* all alone
hearing the coal trucks on the railway line,
the pit to power station wagons beat
a metre as my eye moves down to *Sweet*
on the menu that I've studied countless times,
my head on coal trucks and on coupled rhymes,
and, there, added in purple print, I find
a mouthful of assonance to tempt my mind,
but not my tastebuds, knowing that only
the leisurely, the literary, or the lonely
or some passing, half-pissed plaiting of all three,
Saturday in Donny, and tonight that's me,
notice, of all things in the hopping town
with disco birds and desolate bridal gown,
the Union flag garrotting the flagstaff,

cracking crosses over girl gangs, frozen stiff,
but cackling and cramming the jam-packed pub
or past the bouncers to the throbbing club,
with midriffs, thighs and shoulders, bare and blue,

or Chef's special: melon balls in *Malibu*.

Suspensions

The heave and rattle of the freezer trucks
hauling their rot-prone loads across the Tyne.
That black mid-river in its state of flux
Durham/Northumberland's dividing line.

No boundaries seem fixed. It's all in flow.
From bed we hear the bridges' constant hum.
I count from out of night's continuum
the FRIGOSCANDIA and FRIGORIFICO
from Tarragona or from Bergen docks.
My eyesight's still not bad. You're quite impressed.
I also see both church and Customs clocks,
give or take five minutes, say get dressed.

I wind both windows of my taxi down
to let your smell blow off me down the quays.
I trail your fragrance through the drunken town.

Tonight your essences are on the breeze
suspended in the smells of river slime,
brewery, tarworks, Baltic Flour Mill,
caught in this fixed place, this measured time.

The rushing night air makes my body chill.

My life's one taut suspension, one blind arc!

My semen in your body's not yet dried.
My wife sleeps warm and naked by my side –

my bones, cold girders cast across the dark.

The Beast with Two Backs

Their sulks and marital misunderstanding
were often healed by hot lumbago balm.
I'd seen one or the other cross the landing
to wash the pungent fire off a palm.
What may have kept them coupled through such days
was thinking that the worst of being alone 's
(though you can gratify yourself in other ways)
you can't rub your own back with *Dr Sloane's*.
In the rheumatic North in icy weather
dapper Dr Sloane with waxed mustachios
could keep my parents silently together
touching the parts they'd sooner not expose.

I hear you leave, the gate creak on the hinges
I've meant all year to oil. And now you've gone
and I've got the winter's first rheumatic twinges
and the tube of colourless gel – who'll rub it on?

Grog

Barring my begetting their flu grog-making
was one act that I'd say they'd truly share.
Worth being fluey for, like now, with body aching
that grog it took both parents to prepare.
Neither too much of the one nor of the other:
whisky enough to make a kid's tongue tingle,
honey not too cloying, father, mother,
concoct a brew where both their loves could mingle.
The whisky was Dad's solemn stewardship.
She added honey, cloves and lemon. Steam
perfumed with cinnamon rose as they'd sip
from the spoon they'd stir together with, a team.

My thermos flask of grog 's one way I try,
flu-racked and forsaken, to forget,
when waking drenched and half-delirious, why
the shape beside me 's mine roughed out in sweat.

Mouthfuls

The *Kourtaki* retsina that I buy
from *Kwiksave* costs 2.99.
It helps my nostalgia for Greek sky
when I'm gloomy on the Tyne.

My dad's tastebuds in my head
they've never gone away
and though he's been a longtime dead
he's got to have his say.

Even at 2.99,
he doesn't like retsina
Tastes like bloody turpentine!
Or bloody carpet cleaner!

I quaff it out of barrels though
back where *Kourtaki*'s made
in the Attic town Markopoulo
where they bake a biscuit braid.

This bakery's my dad's ghost's treat.
In Greece he liked this most
though I no longer like things sweet
I go to gratify his ghost.

My father's tastebuds like to go
tasting biscuits I resist
so when I'm in Markopoulo
this bakehouse can't be missed.

The biscuit's got a braided form
made from cinnamon and must
you pick them from the trays still warm
and white with icing dust.

His tongue-tied tastebuds help me speak
in a workplace like his own,
all the proper words in Greek,
words he never could have known.

'They're μουστοκουλουρακια, Dad.'
Nay! Gerraway!
Bloody mouthful for a biscuit, lad!
We both taste one, and I say:

'Cinnamon!' He says: *Too much for me!*
For a foreign biscuit, though, not bad!
In that Markopoulo bakery
I was close to my dead dad.

I dream of him, his spirit comes
from the cold Leeds earth below

spouting μουστοκουλουρακια crumbs
in warm Markopoulo.

Though tarts and stuff are in my blood
the sweetest thing I ever eat
is fruit and never cake or pud
when Dad's tastebuds crave for sweet.

His tastebuds always go AWOL
and leave mine on their own to try
'that cocktail stuff wi' a parasol
to keep all t'bloody ice cubes dry.'

And they'd always go on strike
when I've worked in Japan.
Raw? Nay, lad, tha knows ah like
mi fish from t'frying pan.

I like his tastebuds in my gob
when sampling posh 'cuisine'
then I'm glad they do their job
of saying what they mean.

'All satisfactory, sir, I trust?'
I hear the waiter bray.
Dad's tastebuds have the sauces sussed
and force my tongue to grumble: *Nay!*

78

But so often now I feel them shrink
in a kind of sad defeat
when I neither eat nor drink
anything that's sweet.

Exasperated once I yelled,
'Try something else for pity's sake.
It's time that your baker's tooth rebelled
against craving for sweet cake.'

It's nowt to do wi't'job ah 'ad.
Ah'm bloody glad not to be slaving
ovver t'ovens like ah had to, lad,
but nowt'll stop this craving.

When you go near to summat sweet
it's like a geni's got released.
One crumb of cream-cake you might eat
to me's like a great feast.

Then in a measured and grave tone,
Tha'll soon enough know t'simple truth:
when tha's lying under t'ground alone
Death'll give yer us sweet-tooth.

The Pen and the Gun

There's never a time I use this fountain pen
without I'm haunted by a pigeon's pain.

This pen scrats out the panic that it felt.
It took almost two days dying. All my fault.

My friend Pinhead got an airgun once
and what we did with it still makes me wince.

His mam bought him it when his dad died.
She thought it'd help him not to miss his dad.

It was the thing that Pinhead wanted most.
He had the first few goes, and always missed

the pigeon on his chimney, nowhere near,
so wide the bird stayed basking, unaware.

Then I tried and got, beginner's luck, a hit,
of sorts, with my first ever shot.

It fell in the gutter out of reach and sight
but for its claws that scraped against the slate

Hotlines

Samaritans, *Drug Abuse*, *Rape*, *Homicide*,
the moonrock and the crack ODs,
a man in Florida misdialled and died
reaching the hotline for *Tagged Manatees*.

Measures

Time that's seen my shirt-size swell
from S to M and now to L
won't see it shrink back to petite
until my shirt 's my winding sheet.

Reconnected

Years later, with a desperate need, I phone
and almost pull the flex out of the wall
when the younger voice that answers me 's my own:

Sorry we're not here to take your call.

Realism

What happens when the theatre shuns the word
and an actor strains to show us that he's shitting
's that, strain though he might, from where I'm sitting
I can neither see nor smell a single turd.

Fire & Poetry

i]

The *shakuhachi* 's shattered, the *tatami* 's torn,
the besom's ashes on the scorched moss lawn,
the temple's maples smoking stumps now, but
Basho's ink-stick 's made from soot.

ii]

After 1945 poets could use a new
season word for autumn in *haiku*
along with plum etc they can say:
Hiroshima Day

Wine & Poetry

i]

I only drink white wine, no spirits and no beer.
There've been all told, two wines I couldn't drink
and after just one sip poured down the sink:
one called *President*, the other *Poesia*!

No, sorry, three! A sparkling wine, and Greek,
and called *Lord Byron* but it made me puke!

ii]

One glass and no refill
is life for men,
so keep on pouring till
Death says *when*.

(after Amphis, fourth century BC*)*

Fig on the Tyne

FOR SIANI, ON HER BIRTHDAY

My life and garden, both transforming,
thanks to you, and global warming,
started today to intertwine
tasting my first fig on the Tyne.

When I heard scientists predict
there'd be apricots and peaches picked
in Britain's South, and *pinot noir*
where the rhubarb fields of Yorkshire are,
the pithill *pinot* from lush vines
ripening on demolished mines,
a Rossington *viognier*,
Sheffield *shiraz*, Grimethorpe *gamay*,
fancy made a sun-kissed fiction:
Dionysus redeeming dereliction.
Dionysus! Wishful thinking,
sitting in Doncaster drinking
in Southern sun that lasts all day
a local Donny *vin du pays*.
No sommelier worth his salt 'll spurn
Gewurtztraminer from Wath-on-Dearne!
No longer would we need to traipse
through airports to the lands of grapes.

No more queuing at Heathrow
when we grow all they used to grow.
There'll come a day no Loiner needs
to go beyond the *caves* of Leeds
to sup champagne that's bottled where
they throw their empties in the Aire.
The South creeps Northwards, some say sweeps,
swapping *Beaujolais nouveau* for neaps.
This vision of Yorkshire by the Med
no doubt won't come till I'm long dead.
Torridity in Tyne and Wear
won't come till I'm no longer here.
Predictions for this land of plenty
start, at the soonest, 2020,
which is cutting it a wee bit fine
if I'm to bask beside the Tyne.
Sometimes I have to fantasize
I'm living under bluer skies,
but today I had a little sign
here in Newcastle-upon-Tyne.
Not just that this year's birds are late
leaving the North-East to migrate,
they linger, O they're welcome, they
still sing for me at break of day.
Some prophets that I've read believe
there'll come a day the birds don't leave.

The sign I mean was true but small
and grown against my garden wall.
If the scientists' prediction
isn't all just wishful fiction,
I thought once, why, if Leeds grows wine,
can't I grow a fig tree on the Tyne?
Why not, if the River Aire's
going to wind through wine hectares,
assume the scientists really know
and plant something that needs sun to grow,
more sun than usually comes its way
in Newcastle or Whitley Bay,
and here, on Tyneside, I'll install
a fig on my least sun-starved wall,
and wait for global warming to produce
figs oozing with full taste and juice.
'Fig trees don't grow in my native land'
wrote Lawrence, when his work was banned.
The climate 's changing, figs do grow
(and franker paintings go on show!)
though not like San Gervasio,
where the starved Midlander Brit
found figs as 'fissure', 'yoni', 'slit'.
All those eyesores and black spots
bulldozed flat in his native Notts,
wait the creeping South's advance
to metamorphose into France.

The climate he was restless for
would come up to his own front door.
I tell him now, the man who grew
one Northern fig, that it's not true:
If you want figs, stay put in Notts,
trust global warming, you'll have lots.
In parts of Europe blessed with sun
I've picked hundreds. Now, here, one.
I've roamed about in similar fashion
seeking Southern fruit and passion.
His restlessness fed into mine
though I've always come back to the Tyne.
Though my life 's been a different story.
I've been 'ο ποιητης' and 'Il Signore'.
Places where he used to go,
Italy, New Mexico,
I've also been to, half-inclined
to leave everything at home behind,
then on Guatavita's shores I found
gold everywhere just on the ground.
I come to El Dorado and I find
exactly what I'd left behind!
Too busy being Pissarro
ever to let my garden grow
anything but those tough weeds
I've known in Newcastle or Leeds,

this gold I came to look upon
with an 'O my America' of Donne,
this El Dorado in my head,
when I found it, only led,
after all the searches I got high on
to the El Dorado dandelion.
That was my discovery,
poet/Pissarro of the *piss-en-lit*!
All that we search for when we roam
is nowhere if not here at home.
I picked one for you, and pressed the head
of that Andean piss-a-bed,
and now this one fig I discover
I want to share with you, my lover.
I never thought that it would grow
when I planted it ten years ago.
I decided this was what I'd do
about the same time I'd met you.
I watched it grow and much away
feared it'd die, but now, today,
September 20, '99,
your birthday, love, here on the Tyne,
not flooded yet in Grecian sun,
I picked one fig from it, just one!
I picked the first fig that I'd grown
but tasted its sweet flesh alone,

when I'd wanted, O so much, to share
the fig with one who wasn't there,
you with whom I hope to see
years of figs from that same tree,
I'd wanted here to cut in two
one half for me, one half for you,
to celebrate the first sweet sign
of global ripening on the Tyne
and with the first of my Tyne figs
celebrate you're 46!

I never thought the tree would root
let alone produce a fruit,
I've seen it, like our love, survive
from when you were only 35.
That's almost the length of time it took
to pick this first ripe fig to suck.
My heart too has felt the South,
that puts this fig into my mouth,
warm my heart's North at a time
life's forecast as a colder clime,
and, in the heart's depths, it renewed
love in life's last latitude.
And now today you're 46
and far from the first of our sweet figs.

I've watched it ripen from where I sit
at the kitchen table candle-lit.
I've watched it ripen at each meal.
Facing the autumn now I feel,
as reflected candle on the wall 's
flickering, licking the fig, like you my balls,
so lost without you, that I've plucked
the sweetest fig I've ever sucked.
Such flavour, sweetness! Half 's a feast
though ripened in the chill North-East
ripened through gales and CFCs
warming the globe a few degrees,
and by the shredded ozone layer
and, I confess, my loving care.
(Because my fig tree 's far from Greece
I protect it now with garden fleece.)

I ate my half and then thought yours,
like kids leave cake for Santa Claus,
should be left out on a plate all night
with the half-burnt candle left alight,
so tomorrow, when I woke, I'd know
you'd come to me from Tokyo,
where, as I picked, you'd been performing
among typhoons born of global warming
Goneril in Shakespeare's *Lear*.
But I know you won't be here,

to share the fig picked from my wall
with a ripeness that we know is all.
But so it wouldn't go to waste,
and longing for my favourite taste,
just as Kent said his *Alack*
(Act V, scene iii) I ate the black/
deep ruby bit I'd left for you
just as your corpse came into view.
May the both halves that I've eaten,
like 'an ounce of civet', sweeten
my imagination when I brood
alone on this bleak latitude,
trying to make my simple rhyme
obey the weight of this sad time,
but honour, too, rare days of joy
that death or distance can't destroy.
In Japan your curtain falls
and all the corpses take their calls.
Happy birthday! I'd raise a glass,
if those prophecies had come to pass,
of Bradford bubbly or Leeds *Mumm*,
though unhappy that you couldn't come,
being borne with Regan on a bier
as the deaths piled up in *Lear*,
to the sweetest woman that I've known
most welcome to the figs I've grown.
Next September if you're freer,

and raised from the corpse-pile of *King Lear*
we'll celebrate your birthday here
with storm-ripened fruit. 46
leaves life enough for future figs,
and I still hope to suck a few
though this year I turned 62!
May whatever 's left in yours and mine
bring figs like my first fig on the Tyne.